# LOVE LETTERS TO THE HOME OFFICE

Typeset in Sabon LT Std

Edited by David Ethier

Typesetting and publishing by UK Book Publishing

UK Book Publishing is a trading name of Consilience Media

www.ukbookpublishing.com

ISBN: 978-1-910223-06-2

# *Preface*

**This project is very special to us all.**

Through creating this book, we have met some extraordinary people who are doing extraordinary things purely in order to do something that all human beings have in common: to love, and to love freely.

From the outset, we have aimed to invite others to this cause. Our goal is to welcome, not admonish. To seek change through unity, not isolation. To love, rather than hate.

*Love Letters to the Home Office* is a book of love stories written by people affected by the 2012 Family Immigration law. This law means that our human rights - specifically our rights to live in the UK with our families - are now dictated by how much we earn.

We have met some amazing people along the way, who show courage beyond measure. We've been supported by people who heard about the project and then made it their business to support us along the way. One of those people is Steve from the Britcits charity, and we have asked him to write an introduction to explain the impact of the law.

We are grateful to every person who wrote a story for the book. Some of them moved us to tears. Some of them made us laugh.

Every single one of them taught us a new lesson in what it is to be human, and what it is to live a life of love.

The stories contained in this book are a small representation of lives affected by this law. We seek to give voice to those who haven't had one, to allow their words to touch your heart, and to give resonance to what may otherwise seem to be an ephemeral idea existing on the fringe of our national community.

The effects are real, tangible, and are occurring in the here and now.

We have deliberately chosen to omit surnames. This law has, in one way or another, affected everyone that has contributed time and talent to this book. We believe that the choice for anonymity results in a product greater than the sum of its parts. It symbolizes the fact that we – the authors and audience – are all in this together. As equals, we have a responsibility to seek justice – together.

*– Abbi, Jason,* and *Katharine Rose*

# *Introduction*

I am delighted to support this wonderful, amazing initiative.
On 9th July 2012, the government introduced new immigration
rules which, consequently, wound up dividing families of British
citizens and instituting unprecedented intrusions into the privacy
of both citizens and their loved ones.

The most significant change is represented by a new income
requirement: £18,600 per annum to bring a non-EEA spouse
or civil partner into the UK. The requirement rises to £22,400
for a spouse and non-EEA citizen child and by £2400 for each
additional child after that. The onus is on the British partner to
demonstrate this income; the spouse's income is not considered.
As a result, there are British housewives, househusbands, and
retirees living in de-facto exile across the world despite the fact
that their partners earn more than £18,600 per year, and this
includes families with British citizen children.

Third party sponsorship is no longer allowed. Young people
starting their careers can no longer get help from kind parents,
whereas savings can be counted – the requirement totals
£62,500.

The evidential requirements, especially for self-employed and
contract workers, are almost opaque and considered onerous
at best. Retired people, who do not need to work, cannot use
property they've paid off as a reason to escape the net.

The process itself is prohibitively expensive and entails a minimum of six to twelve months of separation between families. Those with experience liken it to a trial by ordeal.

The impact of the law has been studied. Oxford University's Migration Observatory has found that the income requirement alone disqualifies 47% of the *employed* UK population. Of that population, 58% are between the ages of twenty and thirty – the age when people are most likely to form lasting relationships. There is a disproportionate affect on women: 61% of women in employment fall outside the requirement. In Scotland, 48% are under the minimum. That number rises to 51% in Wales, 52% in Yorkshire, and 53% in the north west of England. Even in the wealthiest city in Europe – London – 29% fall short of the requirement.

But, the income requirement is not the only mitigating factor.

The language requirement for indefinite leave to remain has been tightened; the Life in the UK test has changed its content yet again, and a pass is required in addition to the language test.

The time required for indefinite leave to remain has increased from two to five years, with a check after thirty months. Significant fines on employers have lowered the likelihood of partners gaining employment, slowing the UK economy and placing undue pressure on families.

People are forced to become single parents. Women are trapped in abusive relationships while their immigration status is uncertain. We've seen horrible stories of depression, stress, people forced into poverty, and pregnancies being terminated. Legal aid is under attack, so ordinary people cannot challenge the mistakes of an overburdened system.

The route for elderly dependants has, essentially, been closed.
A response to a parliamentary question indicated that just one
elderly parent visa had been granted in the six months since the
rules were introduced. This aspect of the rules affects higher
earners too; we know of doctors and other professionals forced
to leave the UK to care for their parents. It causes unintended
damage to institutions such as the NHS, which depend on the
work of migrant doctors and nurses.

The human cost is enormous, yet there is an economic cost as
well as people's partners are forced out of the economy. There is
a public health cost as people are reluctant – fearful – to access
health care. Ultimately, there is a moral cost to Britain, which
has compromised its reputation as an example of goodness and
decency.

The campaign that became BritCits began with two friends –
Sonel and Steve – meeting for the first time in August 2012.
In direct response to the new rules, we decided to take action.
Each day, we come face to face with the impact of these rules;
we see husbands divided from wives and parents from children.
It is hard and painful work, but also rewarding. We believe it's
important.

The salient theme is that these rules affect all British citizens.
The affect on one group – migrants – has translated into a
compromise of the rights of all British citizens, from working
class to middle and high earners with overseas partners.

Our work is varied. We give voice to those affected, shore up
resources for help, build solidarity amongst divided families,
endeavour to find solutions, lobby politicians and media, and
connect with other campaign groups inside and outside the
immigration sector. Above all, we provide a platform for those

who have been mistreated by their own government.

Britain is a global country, with a global future, in a world where family members can literally come from everywhere. In the words of Martin Luther King Jr, *The arc of the moral universe is long, but it bends towards justice.*

This book tells a mixture of stories – some heart-breaking, some hopeful. The campaign goes on, and will continue so long as there is legislation that interferes with the natural course of human – family – life. The laws are unsustainable and immoral.

Enjoy the book. And support the campaign!

- *Steve*, Trustee, BritCits (britcits.com)

# LOVE LETTERS TO THE HOME OFFICE

❋ ❋

**I suppose we are the lucky ones.**

Our relationship was born out of being apart. We spent little time together in that first year, but it taught us how to communicate. Since then, he has become the one person with whom I can share anything. No one listens like he does. Even to the little things – like a story of a new pair of shoes – he listens.

And then I listen. His troubles at work, the coffee he regrets having had that day, or the fact he did his laundry.

In the beginning, listening was all we had; now it's our strength. The separation gave us a bedrock foundation. In the two years since, we've carved out time to spend together – to continue building.

Scuba diving in Bora Bora, zip lining in Alaska, dancing at a luau in Hawaii, riding elephants in Bali, swimming with dolphins in Mexico, watching a Russian ballet in St Petersburg, climbing a waterfall in Norway – all events the two of us have treasured, together. But with each adventure, there are always goodbyes. Ours have been countless. We don't cry – at least, not in front of each other. I save my tears until he is gone.

Arrivals, however, are a different story. No matter the country, it's always the same: waiting, watching, thinking *that's him* – only see it's someone that resembles my love, calming myself down, and repeating the process several times again. But, then I see him and can't contain myself; I run. He responds with the smile that asks, *What is she doing* as I leap into his arms. Tight hugs, lots of kisses, and tears – yes, tears – as we welcome each other back to this gift of a moment.

These are the moments where our love shines. This is when I can stop the countdown clock that's in my head, on my wall, on my computer – the clock that says when we will be together again. These are the moments where nothing matters other than the fact that he is here, in the same country, holding my hand. The hand that now has an engagement ring on it.

We walked into this relationship with our eyes open; we knew that our immigration process would be a challenge. We decided to apply for a UK visa. We haven't spent this much time apart since our first year together. We knew that would be the case, but it doesn't make it any easier. Yet, we've done it before – we can do it again.

I suppose we are the lucky ones.

\* \*

David and I met over nine years ago; we've been married for almost seven years. We often joke about how well our marriage works, as we seem to spend most of our time living in different countries, thanks. In the last three years we have had only two visits.

The first one was for six months when I travelled to the UK from Canada. Our intention was for me to live with my husband; however the UKBA changed the rules while I was in the country. Under the new rules, my husband did not meet the financial requirements for me to remain as his wife. I was no longer allowed to apply for a Spousal Visa while in the UK. I was forced to return to Canada.

The second visit was for half an hour in a detention visiting room. I had come to visit my husband, but was refused entry at Gatwick airport. I am a Canadian Citizen who does not require a visa to enter the UK; however with new changes to immigration comes a renewed zeal in Entry Clearance Officers. They were not convinced I would leave the UK after my visit and decided to refuse me entry. I was detained, like a criminal, until my flight back to Canada. David was only allowed to visit me in the detention centre visiting room. What can you talk about in thirty minutes, surrounded by guards and other detainees? How are you expected to feel? In the end, talking was substituted with cuddles and crying.

With the words 'you are no longer allowed to enter the UK

without a spousal visa' ringing in my ears, we went back to the drawing board. David has children, so it is essential for him to remain close to the home. At the moment, there is no way for us to be together while he is living in the UK. We are now exploring the option of us moving somewhere in the EU to be a couple. Our journey continues and we will fight on until we are able to live together.

Our family motto is *Happily Married Unhappily Apart...*

\*\*

'You could always get married.'

It was meant as a joke, spoken by a cheeky uncle from the comfort of a plush armchair in his sister's warm living room. It was one of my early visits to Calum's relatives in Wales, not too long after we'd started going out. We had been talking about my plans after university and the fact that after September 2013 I would have little reason to be in the UK. My visa would expire in January 2014.

That was – and probably still is – commonly held wisdom. *Get married and solve all your visa issues!* And why would anyone question such a belief? It just seems so blindingly obvious that a couple, once married, should get to be together.

That joke feels like a lifetime ago now.

It's been a ride since then. Like any other couple, we've had our ups and downs, but at the end of the day, we always knew we wanted to be together.

We're lucky in many ways. We're young. We're qualified. Neither of us have children or dependants. Relocating to another part of the world is not necessarily a problem – that is unless their immigration policies are as unreasonable as the UK's. In fact, that's what we've done: I'm back in my home country of Singapore while Calum is working in Abu Dhabi. We'll be back in Scotland for our wedding in July. After that, the only thing we know for certain is that we won't be able to stay in the UK. For as long as this immigration rule remains, Calum will not be able to go home – not if he wants to be with me.

I get that a country needs immigration controls. I support the idea of calibrated immigration policies, ensuring that the country can provide for the people – not just citizens – who live within its borders. We can't keep bringing in immigrants if we don't have the infrastructure and support system to provide everyone with a decent quality of life. I can understand that. I've advocated the same for my own country, which is now grappling with its own immigration policies.

But family migration can't be conflated with all other immigration policies and issues. British citizens have the right to live in their own country; they shouldn't feel like they're being forced out just for having dared to marry someone outside of the EEA. And foreign spouses aren't like other economic migrants who can be told to try their luck somewhere else. We don't want to be somewhere else; we want to be with our husbands and wives.

❉ ❉

**I can't easily describe the love I have for my husband.**

There's the *before*: back where it all began, when that newfound understanding of what love allows was like poetry manifest. It levelled everything in its path. Before, there were no hurdles. Our love transcended imaginary lines; national borders could not confine how we felt about each other.

The *now* is filled with that very same poetry, yet we must prove our feelings to a third party. Thus, we wait.

Yet, now is still a good time. I'm visiting my husband (only allowed a visit) in Glasgow. The little things are nice: time to cook, to wait at home, to revel in the simple joy of a clean kitchen. Of course, seeing my husband when he comes home from work, exhausted, is the best. It is us, together, living in a window of now.

But, I'm genuinely excited for the *after*. The after represents our freedom: a house, our careers, a puppy, a baby, holidays, and – most importantly – the certainty of each other, every day. Our lives come after. I want the poetry of *after*.

For the moment, we exist in the interstice between the words of our vows and the deeds of them. For now, I'll wrap myself in our love. I'll be grateful, knowing I am lucky to have it, while looking forward to *after* – an after where we use our love, brick by brick, to build our lives together.

❊❊

At midnight on Sunday my water broke – pop – a little sound.
My heart began to race. I rang the hospital and they told me to
come in. I picked up my chosen birth partner on the way. In the
car I called my boyfriend, my baby's father.

'Where are you? Are you ok? Are you going to hospital? Good,
call me when you know more.'

They told me I couldn't stay at the hospital. Since I wasn't
in established labour, there was no space for me. I called my
partner again.

'Stay where you are!' he said. 'Even if you have to sit in the café,
just stay at the hospital. It's not safe otherwise.'

I stayed and the hospital kindly gave me a bed in the antenatal
ward. Thank God I stayed. In the middle of the night on
Monday I had an almighty contraction that had me howling
uncontrollably. I was whisked to delivery. If I'd been at home
there'd be no way I would have made it back to the hospital; I
was like a wild animal!

At 11am on Tuesday morning, my precious baby boy was born –
healthy and perfect. I called his dad.

'He's here,' I told him. 'He's 3.2 kilos and looks like you.'

I emailed him a photo of our beautiful boy.

Four months later, father and son met for the first time. We both travelled to Venice and stayed there with my boyfriend's family for two weeks. It was a happy and loving time. Father and son were very taken with each other. I made a promise to myself to fulfil my duty to my son, enabling him to have his father in his life.

We said goodbye at the end of the two weeks.

Daddy left on a ship back to Greece and we left on a flight back to the UK. I was at university, sitting my final year exams. Because my income as a student was not enough to satisfy an application for a visa, he was not able to come with us.

I graduated with an excellent degree in modern languages. My baby boy joined me in my graduation photos, me in my academic gown. It was the proudest day of my life. A few weeks later we were on a flight again, this time to Albania to visit my son's father's family on their farm. We stayed for two months. There was a lot of love and a lot of tears.

I'm thankful for so many things: my child, my health, my abilities. But I'm sorry that my son can't have his father in his life. Who knows what pain my son is storing up for the future. Will he ever understand the truth of it? I don't know.

For now we see Daddy on Skype every day. I read to my son in Albanian with the hope that he will feel connected to his father. As a single parent, I still don't have an income to satisfy the requirements of a visa application. Maybe when my son starts nursery, things will begin to change.

I'm glad that my partner ordered me to stay at the hospital that Sunday night. He knew it was the right thing for me even from

1,500 miles away. He's done his bit in supporting me in the best way he can. We try to be kind to each other and remember that neither of us has chosen this situation. By focusing on our son we are able to get through each day knowing – hoping – that things will get better in time.

✱✱

**I have travelled and worked in many countries. I have experienced many cultures and met so many great people. But the greatest of all are my family in Peru.**

My wife and my little girls are everything to me; our bond is strong. My wife, Vanessa, is my true love. We have grown together. We have shared values and principles, goals and dreams. We have love, which holds us close together – through the good and bad times.

Olenka-Skya is four and Fara-Patrisia is two. They are becoming more and more confident as the days go on. We are a strong, loving family and we live in a relaxed and encouraging atmosphere.

We wanted to bring our children up experiencing both our cultures, but I had no choice but to leave Peru in July 2013 because of financial difficulties.

I talk to Vanessa daily, but Skype is a luxury only available in the city centre, which means I rarely see my children. Sometimes, when I do, Olenka is indifferent, not wanting to talk. Other times, she's excited, saying 'Hola, Papi, vamos al parquet?' Those are the times that fill my heart with joy.

We have cried often, in despair for our future. We have cried over not sharing those magical moments that will never return. Moments gone forever. Moments like my children's first days at school.

I often feel as if no one in this great nation cares. I often think I'm seen as a nuisance, a failure, or just someone who should have made better decisions.

It's in those times that I take solace in Vanessa's words: 'I will always love you. So will your daughters. And, with God's help, we will be reunited as a family. You are the best man I have ever known. Don't lose hope.'

❊ ❊

**My darling, blue-eyed boy! Right from the first moment, we clicked. You called me Futuregirl because I come from New Zealand. We knew straight away that I was to be *your* Futuregirl.**

It didn't take us long to fall in love with each other. Right after booking my tickets to come and see you, I began crossing each day off the calendar. So many days! Finally, the day came, and I started my journey from one side of the world to the other.

I was questioned and made to sit on a bench at the border while they called you – to make sure our stories matched. I spent those minutes – what felt like an eternity – worried that I had come all this way only to be denied the opportunity to see you. When the officer came back, his face had softened. He said you were a nice man and wished us luck.

I looked for you as I stepped into the Arrivals hall. I saw you. You really do have the most beautiful blue eyes! You were on the skinny side then; these days you growl about your weight. To me, you are simply perfect.

We have spent all our days and nights together. All except one: the eve of our marriage!

It was a beautiful winter's day. We had a small wedding with family and friends. Wasn't it perfect? Being your wife means the world to me. We are two halves that will forever be a whole. I love you, my sweet, for all the happiness you bring me.

Forever, I will always be your Futuregirl.

\* \*

**Simo is not just my proverbial 'other half'; he is the other half of me.**

When we met in Marrakech, in February 2012, we had an instant connection. Since then, we've exchanged nearly 5000 emails. After a year of correspondence, I met his lovely family and, two months later, we announced that we planned to marry in Morocco in October 2013.

We are similar in many different ways: we like and dislike the same food; we like and dislike the same kinds of music; we like and dislike the same TV programmes. We love going for walks, hand-in-hand. Strolling on the beach. Lying down and looking up at the moon and stars.

He is scared of dogs. I am scared of cats. We have sworn to forever protect each other – even as we each gently tease one another about our fears.

Our outlooks on life are aligned. We have the same respect for family and the utmost respect for each other's religion and culture. Simo wants to learn better English and I want to improve my Arabic. We have agreed this will be part of our married life together.

We want to learn and grow and live together. We don't drink alcohol or smoke. We aren't big partygoers; we just want a quiet, peaceful life that we can share. Together. We laugh at the same things and we love our ever-increasing collection of private jokes. Believe me, when we are together, we laugh a lot!

When we walk side by side, we have the same stride, and we have matching feet. We are the same height, have the same dark hair, the same eye colour – we even look similar.

We love each other with equal intensity and passion. Together, we are one unit; apart, we are incomplete.

\* \*

My husband and I met online. He is from the UK and I am from the US. I finally met him in person, and we fell in love not long after. The feelings I have for my husband are indescribable. I can't picture my life without him. We Skype every single day.

I get butterflies in my stomach every time I get off the plane and meet him at the airport. Thank God we don't have kids yet because it would be so much harder. I would be a single mother.

He's coming to see me in June and I can't wait!

\* \*

**I had always dreamt of my perfect wedding day. How special I felt! To finally be united with my loved one was a dream come true.**

I met my husband in Pakistan and we got married there. Two weeks after my wedding, I had to come back to my job in England. I cried on the entire trip to the airport on the day that I left him. I couldn't let go of the thought: *when will I see him again?*

It has been a year since I left, and I have not seen my husband once since then. I miss him day and night. My life is torn apart; my heart is torn in two. I am not able to share my love with him like so many others do.

I shall never wish this upon anyone. How could it be a government's policy to keep me from living a happily married life?

❈❈

**I have been away from my husband for two years. I am not truly happy because this law is keeping my husband and me apart. Moreover, I have to wait for months for a hearing date.**

Why has this happened? The consequences of this law are loving husbands and wives living in perpetual separation. It causes hardship on individuals, marriages, and families. Please, can this law change as soon as possible?

\* \*

We have been married since June 2013, yet a common theme of our marriage is tears. Each time I return home, I must do so alone, leaving her behind.

The right to enjoy happy days with my wife has been stripped from me.

I am reminded of her tears instead of the moments I hope to share with the love of my life: telling jokes in the kitchen; snuggled, watching movies; sleeping in the same bed; talking, laughing, chasing each other around the garden; falling deeper in love each day.

The home office took this from us. My income is over £19,000. I have applied twice, yet still I wait. I have spent over £2,000 just on application costs and over £10,000 on travelling to meet my wife every few months. All while paying my taxes, my rent, all my travel expenses...

I just don't know. I wonder if they have families. Do they not have wives that miss them? Do they not want to be parents? Even if they don't, I do and my name is **human**.

✳ ✳

**It's been eight years since I first met that sweet, fiercely intelligent, young woman in London. We may not have known it at the time, but it was a night that changed both of our lives forever.**

It's been seven years since that same petite, strong, young woman met me again in my new home. She took me under her wing and helped me survive. I was a callow new arrival in her proud and ancient country.

It's been five years since we married; a decision that feels just as right now as it did all that time ago.

It's been almost two years since our beautiful daughter, the light of our lives, was born. That was the moment that bound us together irrevocably, and gave new, urgent meaning to our lives and our relationship.

It's been a year and a half since we made the decision to come home to England, at long last.

Finally, after a long, hard struggle, we are coming home – together – as a family.

✽✽

**I had no idea that rekindling an old friendship would lead to such change. That was four years ago.**

Emelie and I corresponded via computer and messenger services. She had a quirky sense of humour and a wit so quick that it kept me on my toes. Our conversations were always thought-provoking, changing the way I saw the world. Neither of us began by looking for romance, but what started out as laughter and friendly banter blossomed into a relationship.

I knew little of Manila other than that it was in the Philippines, where the legendary Muhammad Ali had fought Joe Frazier when I was a teenager. My education rapidly developed. I grew fascinated by everything related to the Philippines, but Emelie was even more enchanting. I soon realised that I was falling in love.

The sudden death of my father caused me to re-examine what I was doing with my life – was I taking advantage of the precious time I had been given?

Although I had travelled around the world as a professional trumpet player, I had never made a long distance trip by myself. It wasn't enough to stop me from making plans to visit Emelie in the summer of 2011. Emelie had been sent to the island of Cebu for a temporary work project; I decided upon a split vacation between Cebu and Manila.

I stood outside the Cebu airport, filled with questions and uncertainty. Anxiety dissolved as I turned my head to meet the most radiant smile I had ever seen – the same smile that continues to melt my heart to this day. Her serenity and beauty held me spellbound as I tried to take in the familiar lilt of her voice. We moved to embrace and – in that instant – I knew I would always love her.

After a few months, I returned to Manila to reside with Emelie until May 2012 when we made a trip back to England for a visit. It wasn't too hard to say goodbye when she returned to work in Manila, because I assumed it would be a short separation.

I did not realise that my heart would be ripped apart on 9th July 2012.

We have but few days in our life to tell those around us we love them. Time, simply, runs out. For me, life is for living and loving. Both have been denied me because I fell in love with a beautiful woman from the South Pacific.

\* \*

**We spent a winter meeting for breakfast, whiling away entire mornings in coffee shops – all under the pretence of him teaching me Mandarin. It became obvious – to everyone except us – that we had become inseparable.**

It was after I returned to the UK for the Christmas holiday that we realised we meant more to each other. Although we were eight hours apart, we spent the holidays keeping strange hours in order to Skype each other regularly. It helped us feel closer during the long weeks spent 10,000 miles apart.

\* \*

**My name is Helen and I'm a British Citizen. My husband's name is Shawn and he is from the USA.**

Every time I get ready to fly to the United States, I get sick with nerves and excitement; I can't help but run to the bathroom multiple times before leaving the house.

I feel sick all the way there, but when the plane lands and I walk down that corridor to see my wonderful husband waiting for me, all my sickness and worries disappear in an instant. I rush into his arms and we both hug and cry and kiss. And I feel whole again.

Shawn isn't just my husband. He is my best friend, my soul mate. He is what keeps me going when times are hard. He can make me laugh no matter what our circumstances are. There are no words to describe what we mean to each other. It's like we are two halves that fit together perfectly in every way.

I miss you, my love. There is no better feeling in this world than when I look into your eyes and see *you*.

✳ ✳

**I have known my husband for four years. We recently got married.**

I can't earn £18,600 because I am in full-time education at university. I don't understand why the law says I should live without my husband; surely it should be changed.

I cry every day, missing the love of my life. I miss the joyful life I spent in his country for only a few months. I want him and need him with me. I can't simply move to his country.

I know many people are in the same situation as me. The UK should be treating the people who live here with care, helping us to create successful lives.

✳✳

I was four months from graduating with a degree in psychology, with a post-graduation job secured, when I collapsed one morning at university. Shortly after, I was diagnosed with ME, a debilitating and life-changing condition. Before the illness, I had been a full-time student and athlete. Suddenly I couldn't walk or eat or speak coherently. Following my diagnosis, my partner, Ashley, died. I was grief stricken and lost.

In the wake of these two significant events, my friend Courtney was amazing, supporting me both through my illness and the death of my former partner. We grew closer and began to speak to each other every day. It was vital to have someone in my life who understood my condition, supported me through the loss of a friend, and with whom I had so much in common. For the first time in a long time, something was going right for me.

Courtney and I swapped messages, photos, phone and video calls throughout my recovery, as I learned to manage ME. She eventually came to the UK for an extended trip. Despite having done nothing wrong, she was grilled by the border staff; it terrified her. It was an awful start to what was supposed to be a bright spot of happiness for the two of us. Nevertheless, after hours of waiting, we met and embarked on an amazing visit. Courtney was a glimmer of hope after so much heartbreak.

In 2014, I mustered the strength to journey to the USA after years of illness. I was exhausted but pleased to be with my girlfriend, even if I did spend most of the time indoors. Before returning to the UK, I asked Courtney's mother if I could marry her daughter. She welcomed me with open arms.

Despite her mother's warmth, I was nervous about proposing to Courtney; I imagine anyone on the brink of such a question experiences similar butterflies of anxiety. We took a drive to the Alexander Springs in Florida and, although my illness doesn't allow me to stand for long, I went into the springs and asked a surprised Courtney to marry me.

She was over the moon: we were best friends, lovers, and each other's rock. Her mother sent us to a restaurant to celebrate. When we returned, we found a personalised engagement cake decorated with our names in my favourite colour.

My mother and I began to plan the wedding once I arrived in the UK. Within a few weeks, I was taken ill and admitted to hospital. Another virus was confirmed and, as I have an awfully low immune system, I was kept in. I was scared of not being able to walk again, and Courtney was not with me.

My friend contacted Courtney in the USA. She was beside herself and desperately wanted to come to the UK to be with me. But we were afraid that border control would send her home and we would struggle to see each other after that. The following week I was discharged. Despite agonizing pain, I was pleased to be home, but knew that being without Courtney was not good for my health.

Then a letter from the government arrived: despite my condition, I had been denied PIP support. I felt very alone, with no income and no help from PIP. Even once we are married, Courtney cannot move to the UK because I do not have the income. No consideration is given to the financial situation of my family, who will provide me with financial support once I finish my degree. In terms of my health, I am currently better off in the UK, but not without Courtney. We are heartbroken; despite our clean criminal records, savings, and help from family, we cannot be together. Each direction I turn, the government rejects our relationship.

Courtney works, making headway towards becoming a veterinarian. I am finishing my degree and have the ability to work from home. Currently, I face the reality of being forced to move abroad or leave her; I'm not able to be with my wife. Yet, we wish, desperately, to build a family and care for each other here – in the UK.

\* \*

**When UKBA first refused my application to stay with my husband in the UK in August 2013, I was devastated.**

I felt more confident in February 2014, when I sat, in the first tribunal, in front of an immigration judge and UKBA barrister. I knew my intentions were pure and that I was speaking the truth. I grew scared when the barrister spoke to my husband – in a particular tone of voice – rhetorically stating that, 'once someone is an alcoholic, they are always an alcoholic'. I wasn't afraid for myself; I was afraid for my husband.

I never dreamed that I would fall in love, not at my age. I was forty-one, finishing my NVQ level two and three, and eagerly anticipating returning home to my kids. But, one afternoon, I was cutting the front lawn with a pair of scissors. Strange, I know, but my husband stopped and offered to help me. From that day, both of us knew we were meant to be together. We have ups and downs as any other couple does, but we always come out victorious.

Once he was sure I was the right one for him, my husband confided in me that he had struggled with depression and alcohol dependency. It helped me understand why, in the beginning of our relationship, he would sometimes close himself off from the world (and me). I stood beside him, supportive, believing he could overcome. Together, we conquered his illness.

My husband started his own business, installing fencing

and patios, in May of last year. He is excellent at his work.
The business is so successful that he hasn't stopped working
since then. I help him by joining him for estimates, delivering
materials, and by doing fencing and laying patios when I am not
at work. For the past four years, I have been a full-time carer in
a residential home for people with dementia.

The joy of seeing my husband happy, contented, full of energy,
and thinking of a good life ahead makes me happy. 'I feel
normal,' he says. 'I moved from Essex to Yarmouth with a
suitcase and ten pounds in my pocket. Now I have an incredible
wife, a successful business, family, friends, the respect of the
community, a truck, and a car in the driveway. But, to turn my
life around only to be told by your country that they don't want
you is a kick in the stomach!'

＊＊

There was a Canadian girl who grew up scared and lonely. Years of abuse made her afraid to trust others. By thirty, Toni thought she would be alone forever, never having real friends, never knowing the closeness of family or true love. She decided to sacrifice her own happiness and live for her children from a broken relationship.

There was a Welsh boy who worked hard without a lot to show for it. Craig was a kind person, yet always found he was in relationships which took advantage of this kindness. Craig decided to put his children from a broken relationship before his own needs, resigning himself to being alone.

Little did Toni and Craig know that 4,129 miles across the ocean was the answer to their prayers. One fateful evening a simple introduction changed their lives forever. Instant messages became emails, emails became phone calls, and hours and hours of phone calls became the vacation of a lifetime.

As Craig walked out of the airport, Toni saw her future walking towards her. Their friendship grew into a deep and everlasting love; an unbreakable bond unlike anything Toni had ever thought possible for her. When Toni received her fiancée visa in January 2005 it was the happiest she had ever been in her life – until July 1, 2005, when they vowed to love one another for richer or poorer, in sickness and health, until death do them part. 'What God has brought together let no man put asunder.' They thought their lives would now be perfect. They were wrong.

After years in the UK, they moved to Canada so Toni could finish university. Craig found being away from his children and aging parents too difficult. He returned home to find work and, by July 2012, everything was set for their life back in the UK. However, the immigration rules had changed. Craig's wages did not meet the new income requirement. They were devastated.

On July 1, 2013, Craig and Toni's eighth wedding anniversary, Toni awoke, sad and hopeless. But photos and old letters helped her realize today was not a day to be sad. She picked up a pen and wrote to her beloved husband:

*Craig, you have no idea exactly what you mean to me. Our relationship started as a friendship, the first true friendship I have ever had in my life. When I look at you and our eyes connect, you instantly fill my heart – my soul – with love. You make me feel whole. The love, friendship, and future you give me are more than I ever hoped or dreamed for. You selflessly became Dad to my children, treating them as if they were yours from day one, something my kids never had. You are everything to me: you are my best friend, my other half, my husband. You truly saved me and, for this, you are my hero. You have given me everything I could ever want and I will be yours forever and always. I love you eternally.*

✽✽

**I am a British citizen who is currently married to another British citizen.**

I have always been a taxpaying professional. I am a doctor from a non-EU country, currently serving in the NHS, working and studying towards becoming a Specialist Medical Professional. I had almost become a Junior Doctor, but had to sacrifice that to look after my six-year-old daughter, who is currently in her country of birth (non EU). My daughter is from my first marriage. My ex-husband is not on the scene; he disappeared the moment our daughter was born.

Since her birth, my daughter has been looked after by my parents. It has taken years to assemble reams of paperwork from both countries to be in the position to apply for my daughter's visa. Every year, since her birth, I have travelled back and forth between the two countries many times – to visit her and to arrange the documents. Last year, I was finally able to apply for a UK Visa for my daughter to join me as a 'Non-EU Child of a British Citizen'.

After few months, the Visa was refused. I was shocked, frustrated, and it almost brought me to breaking point. We couldn't eat or sleep for several days. It took weeks to digest the news, try and understand the refusal reasons, and begin taking corrective measures.

It seems that we are yet another family affected by the infamous

£18,600 Financial Requirement rule. We are an unfortunate side effect of this storm. After consulting several immigration lawyers, we have discovered that the Immigration Rule that our child's application falls under does not mention anything about any £18,600 requirement at all. It appears to be a gross mistake, possibly due to the high profile of the Family-Settlement requirement of £18,600. Our case, although entirely different, was treated in the same context.

The Home Office Officer dismissed my husband's Statement of Sponsorship, his salary, savings, and home-ownership. Our joint household income is several times the £18,600 rule. We were in disbelief to find that my husband – my daughter's stepfather – is considered to be a 'third party'. He attached an emotional declaration to the application, enunciating his commitment to support his wife and stepdaughter, yet it apparently made little difference when the Home Office Officer was considering 'The Best Interest of the Child'.

Unity is a pillar of marriage, yet our joint income and savings have been disqualified. Raising a child is a pillar of marriage, yet my husband and I are not considered a family unit. Do we not have the right to decide what is best for our daughter? How many others face the same reality?

We are scared. Our fear extends to the possibility that we have been 'marked', which could affect our daughter's future immigration attempts. We are scared for her wellbeing when she asks, each day, when she'll be allowed to come and stay with us. We fear that her prolonged weariness and longing will have lifelong consequences.

Her upbringing and education has already started to be severely compromised. My parents' health has begun to rapidly deteriorate. Our situation could take months, maybe years to resolve, and they are living with the idea that their grandchild may never be able to join her family. Their question remains the same: who will look after the child if they die?

We can, of course, join the long queue of appeals, but we don't have the luxury of time.

Despite spending recent months working around the clock – consecutive night shifts for days on end, to the detriment of my health and marriage – to reach the £18,600 goal, I have decided to fly out of the UK to join my daughter. Like any other parent, I know that my child is the most important consideration and, thus, have abandoned my job, education, house, and husband to be with her.

Consequently, I have given up on hopes of fulfilling the financial requirement. It means I won't have a steady run of six months in the UK. I've come to believe that even if I met these standards, there'd be something else amiss.

It is heartbreaking to realise that as a tax paying, honest, law-abiding citizen, I have fallen victim to my own country's ill-conceived laws. My tax is going towards the same civil department that is keeping my family apart. I am a civil servant myself, working for the critically ill. What if I used an unsympathetic, non-discretionary, 'tick box' approach? Rules exist to avoid confusion, not to cause them.

I am now leaving the rest to God – that and the hope that the Immigration Officer will be having a good day when she or he picks up my application again.

❊ ❊

There's a wee boy in Chandler, Arizona, USA. He's 15 months old and his name is Robert. He has some baby toys but his favourite thing in the entire world isn't a toy. Robert loves his mum's Samsung tablet. He calls it 'Da da' and carries it around the house all the time.

Robert hasn't seen his father since he was 6 months old. The tablet is all he knows of him. They talk on Skype when they can, but there isn't always a good connection; he doesn't understand why his dad is sometimes sad when they talk and play.

His dad isn't in the army; he isn't working overseas; he's not in prison; he's not in hospital. Robert's dad is in the UK, working desperately to get his wee boy back. Robert is a UK citizen, born in Scotland. His dad is a UK citizen and his eight year-old sister has a permanent visa to live in the UK. But they can't because Robert's mum, Jodie, is American.

In March of 2012 Jodie was torn. Her dad, her only parent, had been ill with a serious heart condition for some time when her stepmum called to say that he had been taken to the hospital again. Jodie was terrified that he would die without having seen his grandson. She also wanted a chance to say goodbye. She was living in Scotland with her husband, Gavin, but her dad was in California. At the time, Jodie was working hard to support her husband through university in Scotland. Gavin worked a few hours as a youth worker but Jodie was the financial mainstay of the family. She was coming up to the end of her second two-year settlement visa and would have been eligible to apply for permanent status. She knew that they didn't have enough money saved for that application *and* for tickets to fly to California. She chose the latter.

In early April, Jodie boarded a flight to California with her young daughter and baby Robert, leaving Gavin to finish his degree in Scotland. Before she left, Jodie rang the Home Office and was told that, when necessary, she would be able to apply for a visa to come home from the US 'no problem'. She lived and worked in the US, spending as much time as possible with her dad who, despite his illness, was overjoyed to see his grandchildren. Jodie and Gavin talked about perhaps moving back to the US for a while so that she could be with her dad more, allowing him to get to know the kids. They didn't get that chance; Jodie's dad died in September.

After the funeral, in November, Jodie applied for a new visa to come home to Scotland – the one that would be 'no problem'. She discovered that while she had been helping to care for her dad, the UK Government had quietly instituted new 'family' immigration rules. The time she had spent working and paying taxes in the UK didn't count; since Gavin was the UK citizen, she couldn't apply for a new visa without 6 months' proof of *his* income. Gavin had been a full-time student, entering his final year. He didn't have 6 months' proof of income. Jodie and the children couldn't come home.

Gavin immediately quit university, without graduating, but didn't land a job right away. It took time to put together the necessary documents, bank statements, proof they would have a place to live, and proof that Robert was a citizen. In the meantime, Jodie and the children became nomads. They roamed through several states, staying with various relatives, moving Robert's sister from school to school – all while Gavin worked 70 hours per week to put together proof of the necessary income level. Without his degree, Gavin had to take low-paying jobs, which required him to work a punishing schedule of 12-hour night shifts to make the money. But he was absolutely determined to do it. They kept in touch via late night phone calls and Skype. Christmas was hard.

The situation this family found itself in was not of their making. They are not 'scroungers' or 'benefit tourists' with a nefarious plan to come back home so they can 'sponge' off the UK system. They just want to work and have a good life like anyone else. Before Jodie's dad was taken ill they were well on their way to doing it. Jodie had worked hard in Scotland, supporting her husband and keeping the family going. Gavin was just a few months away from graduating. Two out of the four members of their family are UK born yet they have been kept apart and punished by a law that picks on UK citizens whose only 'crime' is falling in love and marrying someone from outside the EU.

These families are the most vulnerable because they are the only group of immigrants over whom the UK government has complete control; it represents a tiny portion of immigration statistics but one the government has selected. Gavin has missed the first year of his son's life solely because his wife wanted to see her dying father. His family have been forced to be nomads, wandering from relative to relative and state to state. Their home is in Scotland but they can't get back.

Robert's big sister kept telling her dad she wanted a hug and she wanted to see her friends. She wonders if, perhaps, her dad didn't love her any more. She doesn't understand why she can't just come home.

This policy is hardest on the children. How does one explain that Daddy and Mummy love you, but the government says you can't see them? There are no adequate words. And a Samsung tablet is no substitute.

❊ ❊

Depression is not really part of my emotional make-up. I can honestly say, though, that the past year and a half have certainly been tinged with it. Lots of tears of anger, tears of frustration, and, mostly, tears of sadness have been shed.

The year and a half's struggle in Japan that my son, Steve, wrote about in his contribution to this book, was a struggle for us, his family in the UK, too.

It was a sad time. I feared that my son and his family would be exiled forever.

I spent many days worried, saddened, and angered at the thought that my British-born son – and his unique family – wanted desperately to come home, to the UK, but that the British government was stopping them.

The fear is over now. Yoko has been granted her spouse visa and they are coming home in April. We – his family – can't wait!

It will be so good to have the entire family round for Sunday lunch, for special occasions, or, simply, to spend time together. It will be so good to meet up for a coffee or to visit them in their own home. It will be so good for the cousins to get to know each other, to play together.

Sunshine is returning to our family.

✻ ✻

**I noticed that my daughter, Katharine, was making more frequent visits to Europe a few years ago. It wasn't just for work reasons, and she seemed happier, more focused.**

When she told me she was in love with Raco and that they wanted to get married, I was happy for her – but also a tad apprehensive. My only daughter was getting married to a man I had never met and who came from a country I had to search for on an atlas!

I must say, however, that once I 'met' my future son-in-law via Skype, I felt relieved. I had a strong sense that all would be well and that it was very much a love match.

It was sweet when he called me Mum. They were both excited about Katharine's imminent visit and the forthcoming marriage. We had great fun discussing how they would get hold of Katharine's grandma in Yorkshire from Montenegro – via Skype – to tell her the news.

The three months between engagement and wedding were a whirlwind of wonderful activity. I learned as much about Montenegro as I could. My daughter and I shopped for her dress and shoes. We organised flights and hire cars for godparents and friends so that everyone could make the trip for the wedding.

Seeing Katharine and Raco in Podgorica was one of those peak life moments where time stands still. I'll never forget the image of them walking, hand in hand, towards us.

The two sets of families and friends – Raco's and Katharine's –
had a magical time getting to know each other, finding the same
love and support in their counterparts. His grandmother and her
grandchildren hold a special place in my heart. I'm very much
looking forward to seeing them again when I visit this summer.

The wedding was wonderful. My daughter was at her beautiful
best. The love in the air, the warmth and goodwill for the future
of the bride and groom felt tangible.

It would be another eighteen months before they could finally
live – together – in the UK.

It has been difficult to watch how painful that has been for
them. It was sad that my son-in-law was not able to be at my
own wedding in the UK purely because of our own country's
immigration system. Raco finally arrived in the UK three weeks
ago, and having him here to meet my husband, enjoy the English
countryside, have dinner with us, and, of course, to be where he
is meant to be – with my daughter – is *just wonderful*.

❋❋

**On 1 February 2009, I emailed a Canadian girl, asking her if she wanted to be pen pals. I never imagined what would follow.**

Laura and I began by sending hundred-word emails every few days. Then every day. And then *several times a day*. We moved on to speaking in real time via Internet chat for several hours each day, and eventually grew brave enough to talk on the phone. You see, we're both introverts and both of us see ourselves as a bit socially awkward; it's miraculous that we found each other.

In fact, the odds of two seemingly random people from different countries becoming such close friends was all I could think about. Laura and I had fallen in love. I decided to go to Canada for a week. The time we shared far outweighed my unfortunate experience with Canadian border control in Ottawa, trying to explain that I was alone and on my way to see someone I'd never 'met' before. She later reciprocated by flying – for the first time in her life – to the capital city.

We had found love, had visited in each other's countries, and the time came for us to take a leap of faith. Laura left her family, friends, and home to come live with me at university in Aberdeen; she was on a two-year Youth Mobility Scheme visa. The risk was not lost on either of us, yet it worked out wonderfully. It was easy, even, and the two of us wound up going everywhere together.

Two years seemed, in the beginning, like it would last much longer. We got a cat, we did the shopping, we went on holiday. We built a home. She loved the proximity to cities that northern Ontario doesn't have. Laura embraced my Welsh culture as I did hers. The adventures moved our time along at a much faster pace than we imagined. After her visa expired, Laura returned to Canada.

It wasn't until after Laura had returned to Canada because of her visa limitations that the immigration rules changed, testing our relationship like never before.

We've only been together for three weeks since 2010. Despite that, we've been creative, finding new ideas to maintain a long-distance relationship. I have a job, which pays nearly £18,600, so I hope that we'll soon be together again.

Airports have become the most emotionally charged space for us. I associate them, firstly, with anguish and, secondly, with delight. My dream is that I'll never again have to watch my heartbroken love pass through a departure gate with the feeling that I've been split in half, not knowing when I'll see her again.

\* \*

**We shared Christmas together in 2012. It was our last Christmas in the same country.**

We had a beautiful Christmas dinner, just enjoying the time we had together.

Now we talk on Skype every day for hours. We hope to be together, as a couple, one day soon.

We shared our final Christmas together in 2012.

**

**I have been separated from my wife for two years now because of this seemingly meaningless rule. I don't understand the basis for the financial requirement; the UK's national wage is barely over six pounds per hour. It doesn't seem fair.**

Please, for God's sake, change this rule. Next month, my wife will have surgery, yet I can't be there for her. Is it her fault that she is a British national and we love each other?

\* \*

I am a British citizen and I have been married for one and a half years. My wife is Syrian, living in what is now a war zone. I can't bring my wife to the UK. I live with constant worry. I wake, each night, with nightmares.

\* \*

I first met my wonderful husband-to-be while I was working in The Gambia with a charity. My parents introduced us. I reckon they secretly set us up, sending us off to work by ourselves for the entire day.

We spent two weeks working, enjoying each other's company, and laughing together. The first time my mum introduced us, I knew this was different. There was something there; we both felt it – a connection that reaches across two continents and three thousand miles.

Now, fifteen months later, after two more amazing visits to The Gambia, my amazing, gorgeous fiancé and I will be getting married! It will be in April 2014. I will be visiting the smiling coast for the fourth time. My mum, dad, brother, brother's girlfriend, my two best friends, and some other family friends will be joining us for a colourful, sunny wedding in The Gambia.

I am so lucky.

Sal has done all the organizing, and I totally trust that he will make it an amazing day for all of us.

I miss him so much when we are away, and I look at our photos every day. We are in contact all the time, thanks to technology. When I am with him, it feels like my world and life are whole. Even thousands of miles apart, I couldn't imagine life without him.

We have an uncertain future ahead. We don't know when our lives together can truly begin. We will wait for each other, no matter how long it takes. We can't wait until that happens; we look forward to the time we'll have together.

Love you so much, Sal, with all my heart. I will always keep fighting and will never give up, no matter how hard it is, no matter what rules are in our way. *I will never give you up.*

\*\*

Gavin and I have been married for almost a decade. We married in the Church of England what seems like eons ago, but five weeks later, my UK visa expired and I had to return to America. We knew that there was no way for me to renew my visitor's visa so we made the decision for my husband to explore the U.S. immigration route once I was back on home soil. Eleven months of our first year of marriage was spent an ocean apart. It was an experience neither one of us was willing to repeat. We have been best friends and soul mates since the first time we heard each other's voices; being apart for that long was horrible.

In the end, we overcame the distance and my husband finally arrived in the United States, spousal visa in hand. We planned to go back to England someday, making a fifty-fifty deal: some time in my country and some time in his. I would do a postgrad in the UK, let our son spend some time getting to know his British family, and we'd enjoy being an international couple.

We never dreamed that my husband would be exiled from his own country.

In early summer of 2012 I began to research ways for us to return to England. I learned that the rules were going to change in a few weeks, but I didn't give it much thought. I had no idea the changes would make the rules so drastically different. I had no idea that we would fall short of the new income requirement by less than a thousand pounds. I had no idea we would have to have such an excessive amount of savings to make up the shortfall.

Not only were we shocked, but I was appalled. As an American, I had always looked at Britain as a more progressive country than my own. That was my naivety, I suppose. My romanticism. I no longer feel that way. I am appalled that my husband is exiled simply because he married a non-EU citizen and does not meet an arbitrary income requirement. I am appalled because, under these rules, I am a non-person – *my* income, *my* education, *our* assets, and the fact that we've already cleared one country's hurdles, never needing public assistance, counts for nothing.

If we knew then what we know now, I am not sure we would have made that same decision nearly nine years ago.

My heart breaks for our son's grandmother. She wants so much to be a part of his life, but the Home Office says that her own British son doesn't earn enough money to have this amazing family in their country. My heart breaks for my husband who simply wants to spend time with his mum and to have his whole family together again.

My heart breaks.

❉ ❉

**I met my wife five years ago in Seoul. It was our very first day as English teachers, and we hit it off almost immediately. We grew together as professionals and our personal relationship developed into a perfect partnership of opposites.**

We married in June 2012 and had big plans to come back to the UK, initially as students. After graduating, we'd take the next professional steps while, ultimately, starting a family.

Some may ask why we didn't want to start a family in Korea. Doesn't it have one of the highest student pass rates in the world? Doesn't that mean that their education system is one of the best? Not necessarily. In addition, if we were to have a son, he would be forced into compulsory military service. As I have never viewed conscription as acceptable, we made the choice to start our family life in the UK. It was a no-brainer for both of us.

Unfortunately, this was not to be, as we were going to be students. Thankfully, though, Hyun Sun obtained a student visa; we got our qualifications together and spent a wonderful 15 months in the UK (an experience that I can appreciate some couples in similar situations may not have had, though I hope they all do one day).

Hyun Sun had been in the UK on a student visa. I am now writing this letter while she is in Korea, waiting for me, as I apply for jobs here in the UK.

I have actually found a full-time job, with good prospects, working for a UK university – in China. This is great and it means we will get to be together; however we must put our plans for a family on hold.

My wife has been in Korea for two months and the time here has been lonely. I cannot wait to see her smile in person instead of through a monitor.

It is sad that I – and others in our situation – cannot simply settle with our loved ones, in our beloved home country. Every person I tell my story to shows the same incredulous disbelief, saying, 'But you're English!'

All I can say is, 'Yeah, I know.'

✽ ✽

Before I met Chris I wasn't even sure where Wales was on a map. I grew up on a small farm in a rural Canadian town, never imagining that I would fall in love with someone who lived thousands of miles away.

In 2009, Chris and I became pen pals; he taught me about rugby, Welshcakes, and what the sea was like. Our feelings for each other blossomed quickly and we decided to meet in person for one week, which wound up being far too short for me.

I worked hard and saved every penny I earned so that I could apply for the Youth Mobility Visa. I encountered a lot of criticism when I told my family and friends that I was moving to the United Kingdom to live with someone I had known for longer, but had only visited for one week. Neither disapproval nor fear held me back from wanting to be with Chris.

My time with Chris in the United Kingdom felt like a dream. I never imagined that I could feel so happy and complete with anyone. I pestered Chris about getting a cat; although he wasn't initially keen on the idea, he gave in. Her name is Lucy. She is part of the hundreds of happy memories that Chris and I made together. Once my visa ended, I returned to Canada assuming that I would be able to return, starting a life with Chris. That never happened.

I miss him. I miss walking around the park with him, eating ice cream and always giving him the chocolate flake, singing to him, watching him play the piano, and holding his hand. It would be very easy to write about all the pain and frustration I feel about being unfairly separated from Chris. However, after five years, nine hundred emails, one cat, many tears, and the most amazing adventures, I can say that loving Chris has changed me forever and I will love him for the rest of my life.

✽ ✽

My name is Amanda and I am British. I met Candelario at a
friend's barbecue in the Dominican Republic in 2011. I was 47
at the time; Candelario was 39. I wouldn't say I was attracted to
him at first. In fact, getting into a relationship was the last thing
on my mind. He cheekily persisted in attracting my attention,
giving me no choice but to get to know him! I was, inevitably,
taken in by his huge personality and happy demeanour. I've
never laughed so much as when I'm with him. I could not help
but fall for him. I've never felt as strongly for anyone as I do for
Candelario.

Candelario was a delivery driver at the time. I didn't get to see
him on the nights that he worked late. Despite knowing that
was the reality, I'd still be disappointed if he didn't call around.
His earnings were a pittance in comparison to my earnings back
home. He gave most of his salary to support his children from a
previous marriage. He had been separated from their mother for
about three years but endeavoured to be a loving and responsible
father. He had little more than the clothes he stood up in and an
old, battered motorbike. He had lost his parents before he was
thirteen years old. I can't understand how in those circumstances
someone can turn out so well mannered and kind hearted.
Nonetheless, it didn't deter me. I already knew that being with
someone for money and security doesn't always make a happy
life.

When I returned home, our relationship grew stronger. We
would talk on the phone or on the computer each day. I visited

him as much as possible over the next year as the UKBA turned him down for a visitor's visa. I understand it's very hard to get one. Back then Candelario couldn't speak a word of English. We would manage to communicate with the little bit of Spanish I knew and a dictionary that went everywhere with us.

I think we knew we wanted to spend the rest of our lives together from the start. Leaving him at the airport was unbearable. My chest would tighten with panic and I could barely breathe. I had to tell myself that I must have faith and we would be together soon. I remember telling him anything is possible. I was brought up to believe that if you really want something, you could make it happen. However, back then I had no idea what I was going to be up against: the UK government.

I went to see an immigration solicitor about visa applications once we were married, but I came away feeling totally bewildered. I assumed after you were married, your spouse could come to the UK to be with you – now that has all changed. I remember thinking, on the way home, *surely this can't be true.* What the solicitor said sounded more like discrimination and a violation of human rights than a visa application. How could the country I was so proud of treat people this way?

Not being one to give up, I went to work, straight away, on expanding my business. It was a big risk, but it would be the only way I was going to earn the £18,600 required. I feel very fortunate that I had this option, as I know there will be many out there that won't be able to do the same.

Candelario started English classes in the evening. His manager made him do overtime on the nights he had class. I still don't understand the reason why. Maybe it was jealousy. Either way, the long hours caused problems, he rarely got paid for them, and the turnaround between work and class left little time for sleep. Candelario never complained; there was a queue of people waiting for his job and he had children to support.

Finally, we managed to get a visitor visa. We were overjoyed. Candelario arrived in July 2012 into Manchester airport. He had never been on a plane before. We were totally inseparable and, for the first time in over a year, I was living life again. My face said it all: I had a constant smile and butterflies in my stomach each time he walked into the room.

We got married here in the UK in December 2012, against the stipulations of his visa. As his return date was growing nearer, we were desperate to make a commitment to one another. Candelario had to go back home two days after the wedding, but I promised him he would be back with us before he knew it. I was wrong; his quick return was not to be.

There was no doubt in my mind that he would pass the English exam in January. He had continued with private tutoring while in the UK and, from the information from the UKBA and my solicitor, we thought the exam was basic. He was ready. There was some unfortunate news, however: his boss had filled his position. I didn't mind sending him money in the meantime; we were married and soon to be reunited.

When he failed the English exam, we were both disappointed. After investigating, I found that the exam was closer to an assessment of candidates for employers than the simple review the UKBA had led me to believe. It's an intimidating process that puts undue pressure on the candidate, severely affecting an individual's ability to access their true knowledge. When I saw the exam I had to laugh to keep from crying; it was by no means *basic*. My heart went out to poor Candelario – he didn't stand a chance.

Candelario went on to sit the exam another four times over the next eight months. During this time I pulled out all the stops and got him the best tutor I could find. That was £400 a month on top of supporting him, and, with exam fees added, you can imagine it cost me a lot. I remember thinking that his unemployment was a blessing in disguise since it meant he had more time to study. I visited him twice as he was studying, the last time being September. We received his failed exam results whilst I was there. He would hold me tight and entwine his legs around mine in an attempt to never let me go. We both knew that the time would come – as it always does – to say goodbye.

About three or four days before I leave, each time, we will look at one another differently. We know the time is coming. It's like a black wash waving over us. We grow tearful. I will wake in the night with a jolt, shouting 'I can't do it, I can't do it', and he'll hold me and shush me back to sleep. At the airport, there's another panic. I know what to expect. I've no idea how I do this and keep going for more.

It had been two years when I returned home in September. I decided I had finally had enough. Enough of the exams, enough of the credit card bills, enough being without Candelario. If I could go and live in his country I would go tomorrow. I love it there, but unfortunately it's not an option. I have a fourteen year-old daughter who is in the middle of exams, and I would never jeopardise her future. Candelario was becoming depressed. I think he was giving up hope and starting to lose respect for himself. He thrives on work and the unemployment was taking its toll. I spoke to my immigration solicitor. She thought we had given above and beyond and that it was time to put in the application regardless of the English exam certificate. We would explain the circumstances and include reports from Candelario's professional tutors stating how he had developed a good level of

English over the last year.

We hoped that the officials checking Candelario's application would show some compassion for the circumstances, but no, he was turned down in the middle of January 2014.

We are destroyed. I live with the potential of panic attacks every day. I am not sleeping and have to receive counselling to cope with the anxiety. It feels like grieving, yet he is not dead. Sometimes I feel suicidal because I am not in control of the situation. I have no idea what to do next. Candelario feels bad because he knows the affect it's having on my health, and tries to keep his own sadness to himself, knowing that to share would make me feel even worse. Some in my family have suggested I give him up because it is reducing me to a shell of my former self. I think the suggestion is ludicrous. He is my soul mate; I am him and he is me. There is no way I would ever give him up.

✳ ✳

**There are many moments that I want to share about my relationship with my fiancé:**

The first is heartbreak when, in September 2012, we realised that we would be in a long-distance relationship; I had graduated without securing a job in the UK as he finished his work experience in Singapore.

The familiar but still very sharp pain in my chest every time I have to let go of his hand to board a plane.

The pain I feel every time my fiancé is upset and I can't be there for him.

But, then there's the happiness I've felt during all the times I visit him, being able to hold him close, breathe him in and kiss him. Nothing can replicate that warm feeling in my stomach when I'm with him.

However, instead of the pain of separation and joy of reunion we've experienced for the past two years, the moment I really wish to share is one of hope:

It was the day I found out that I had received a second lower class (2:2) degree in law. A recently-graduated foreigner with a 2:2 has no chance of convincing a local employer to sponsor her visa. That also meant that I was rejected from a postgraduate programme I had previously been offered. It felt like a death knell; I broke down. I was fortunate that my friends were there to make sure I didn't do anything stupid.

At that time, my fiancé was on a post-exams trip with his best friend. I didn't know how to break the news to him. I assumed the worst. Losing him would have destroyed me. In the end, I sent him a text with the news and waited for him to arrive home that evening.

Instead of berating me for only getting a 2:2 and jeopardising our relationship, he wanted to keep fighting. He asked if I saw a future for us if we were engaged. I cried 'yes'.

I don't really know how to describe that moment. There was a sense of relief when it became clear that my fiancé didn't want to let me go so easily – and there was a wave of overwhelming, immeasurable completeness. It was a feeling that gave me hope that we can beat the immigration laws and that we can have a future together. We aren't idiots; we both know that the separation will be hard. But we also know that our relationship is worth fighting for.

\*\*

**I have written a love letter from my son, Malachi. He is one year old.**

My Mummy and Daddy met in The Gambia when my Mummy was a volunteer. They fell in love and spent all the time they could together, walking on the beach, watching the sunset, cooking, even cleaning the house. They loved spending time together.

They loved each other so much that they made me! They were so happy, but Mummy had to leave Daddy and come to England to give birth. She was very afraid and she missed my Daddy a lot. Daddy tried to come and see me being born but he wasn't given a visa.

I wanted to meet my Daddy from the day I was born. Mummy told me about him every day and each night we blew him kisses. She tells me he loves me and one day we will all be together.

She took me to meet him when I was two months old. I remember his face at the airport. He was so excited to see me, his son. He danced with me around the airport. It made Mummy cry. Daddy couldn't stop looking at me. He loved me straight away. He took me for walks under the mango trees and for rides in the car to keep me cool when it was hot in my bed. He took me everywhere and was so proud of me.

Then Mummy and me had to come home; it was horrible.

Mummy and Daddy were both crying. They wanted us to be a family, and so did I. I missed Daddy a lot.

Then, when I was 8 months old, Mummy took me to see him again. We were so excited, I couldn't wait for Daddy to kiss and cuddle me again, and I had learned some new things that he had missed out on. I could crawl, I had teeth, and I could say 'Mama'.

It was the best 5 weeks of my life. Every morning I got up and Daddy was there. He carried me on his shoulders to the beach and to see his friends. He read me stories and played ball with me. I loved it when he gave me a bath. We had lots of fun splashing in the bubbles.

While we were there, Mummy and Daddy got married. We all had such a great time. I danced with Mummy and Daddy and they danced together. I thought we were going to be together forever. But then one day we were back at the airport. My fun with Daddy was over again. We don't know when we will see Daddy again because Mummy has to find a job to try and help Daddy to come and live with us.

If I had one wish I would wish that Daddy could be here with Mummy and me. I love Mummy a lot and she looks after me, but I need my Daddy here. For now, we can't be a proper family, but I'm living for the day when Daddy comes to stay forever.

\* \*

**Every Friday my family gets together for a meal. Three generations sit around a table talking, laughing, and enjoying each other's company.**

I look at my parents-in-law. Growing up in the Soviet Union, they never learned English. It seemed almost pointless to them. The cold war appeared unending and, even amongst the Russian intelligentsia to which they belonged, they could not imagine circumstances in which they would need English. Forty years later they struggle to find the words, yet the conversation flows.

For my own parents, who grew up in the West, the possibility that they would share a table with a Russian physicist – someone who had worked on the guidance systems of rockets targeting their homes and cities – seemed just as unlikely. Now, in their twilight years, enjoying the company of their children and grandchildren, what seemed a fantasy has become a reality.

Borders once impregnable have broken down, and the world that was once so limited has opened up, enabling people from vastly different backgrounds to meet, fall in love, and set up families.

Our family has grown over the last few years. Newly born babies enjoy the cooing of their grandparents; older children thrive on the attention.

As another wonderful evening draws to a close, I cannot help but think about the irony that in England – the country of my birth

– I could not enjoy the same family life. My wife's parents are unwelcome.

It is of no importance that they are highly educated, affluent and healthy, or that their children and grandchildren are British. Their Russian citizenship denies them – and us – the right to a normal family life together.

Luckily, our common Jewish heritage means that what I cannot enjoy in the country of my birth, I can enjoy in Israel. But I cannot help thinking how sad it is that those less fortunate than my family spend long nights alone, yearning for evenings such as these.

✳ ✳

My husband is British. I'm an American. We were married in 2000 at Warwick Registry, and I got my spouse visa from the British Consulate in Chicago on the way to our honeymoon. Back then it was a same day service.

I was the director of our limited company in the UK; we did contract work for the government. I was eventually given permanent right to remain.

In 2005, we sold the company to one of our employees, moved to the US, and set up a new company. During that time, my husband earned his PhD, worked for the university, and did contract work for federal and state governments, helping people with disabilities.

Over the years my father-in-law came to visit us twice. As we were on a student's income and my full time job paid our mortgage, we were unable to afford to visit the UK. We maintained contact via Skype.

Following my husband's graduation, he flew to the UK to visit his father. Spending time with his father, seeing how much he had declined with age, my husband felt that we needed to be back in the UK near him. We aren't promised tomorrow. My husband wanted to honour his father by being here for him in his old age.

We sold our home, paid off our debts, and flew our three dogs

and ourselves to the UK in August. My husband returned as
a citizen and I returned as a visitor with a six-month stamp.
We believed, when the time came, we could apply again at the
British Consulate in Chicago. We found out this was no longer
an option.

My husband rented a small cottage on a farm. We purchased a
used car and bought a year's worth of car insurance. We paid to
set up our company: website, SIM cards, marketing. My husband
began to go to network meetings. Everything was out of pocket
since our eight year-old credit rating was too old to qualify for
a loan. He also began to put together a not for profit advisory
service, free for people with disabilities.

I lived with my husband, but was not allowed to work or
volunteer as a visitor. I could not help earn money or spend
time developing the company so that we could meet the income
requirements. It was very frustrating. I helped our former
company to succeed with a lot of hard work and, as a result, we
employed five additional British citizens.

My six months as a visitor was nearing the end when we found
out shocking information: because my husband is self-employed
he would have to submit audited annual accounts to prove
income. Although he had earned over £10,000 in six months,
he wouldn't have the required accounts before Spring 2015. We
were also informed that the Home Office doesn't simply look at
the total earnings. They look at each month. If there is a month
where you earn less than one twelfth of £18,600, they use the
smaller amount to tell you that you didn't meet the monthly-
required amount.

Most know that when starting a company, you don't see an
immediate income. It takes hard work to build from scratch

– especially in a difficult economy – but my husband was managing.

We met with our MP who, although sympathetic, couldn't get anywhere with the Home Office.

I was told to return to the US while my husband continued to work to build the company and meet the required income. Despite having been married for 15 years, and having never asked for a handout, it appeared that the UK didn't care about our marriage, my husband's effort, or our family. The whole thing has been emotionally painful.

If I had returned to the States, I wouldn't be allowed to return to the UK for a year. Americans are only allowed to visit for a maximum of six in every eighteen months. I would be returning to no home, no job, no car, and no money – we had spent our savings to get the company going.

Neither of us has ever signed up for welfare here or in the US. We simply would not. We are hard workers. We would scratch and scrape and find a way to survive without assistance.

I had to be out of the UK by February 14 or overstay and risk being unable to return for 10 years; we began to try to figure out how we could stay together. We are in our 50s and didn't want to be separated. We decided to move to Ireland where we could live together and I could work. My husband could also occasionally get over to see his father and older sister.

After we had bought our ferry tickets and sent a down payment to the landlord in Ireland, my husband was finally offered lecturing work. He was unwilling to stay in the UK without me and declined the job. I offered to return to the States, but he wouldn't hear of it. He loves me and doesn't want us to be apart.

So we are living in Ireland. We hope that someday we can be near Dad. We pray his health holds up through all of this.

❊ ❊

**It is the bit where they turn you down that always tears my heart open the most.**

For me, there was only ever one person who could make that feel okay, and that was the person sitting at the other end of the Skype connection, totally distraught.

It is the bit where you just want to hold each other and find a way to make the hurt go away, but the hurt exists only because you aren't allowed to be together.

This time was different, though. I knew that, somehow, we had a chance. I didn't know what that chance was, yet, but I knew I was going to do everything I could to make it work.

I could see the pain in his face, in his body. I was trying to wait until that subsided before I could work out what was going on. But that pain stays for weeks, in my experience. All the nights of going to bed alone, hurting for the person that you miss more than anything, and waking up each morning into the new realisation that you are alone and you don't have any guarantee of when or even if that will ever change make it hard for the pain to go away.

So, I just ploughed ahead to find out how I could make this work.

His father had found the letter from the Embassy that morning.

It was on the ground floor of their apartment building by the dustbins. The letter was dated nine days earlier; it had been sent standard post, not registered delivery. We later found out that the letter had arrived just one day prior to my husband's father finding it. Each time I tell this story, I think how grateful I am that the letter didn't end up in the rubbish.

The Embassy had kept my husband's passport, writing to him instead of returning it with a rejected stamp inside. He was angry – he wanted his passport back – but I was grateful. I wasn't quite sure why it had happened this way, but it had, and it gave me hope.

He read out the letter. It was the same stuff that we had heard before in two refused holiday visas and one refused marriage visa application. But the terminology was different this time. We were 'On Hold', and the passport had been kept in the Embassy office where the visas are processed.

We had been turned down for financial reasons. Again. This was the second time. This, despite the fact that we had waited to apply until my finances were well over the £18,600 requirement. Both times it seemed that the Officer had misunderstood my paperwork.

The Officer was clear in the letter, although I was referred to as my husband's *husband* rather than his wife! We had been turned down purely because we hadn't provided every single document in the long list required from me as a Self-Employed person.

We had, actually.

In addition to that list of documents, we were introduced to a new list. The 'Employed Income' list contained documents I didn't yet have, since I'm self-employed. You see, one particular organisation puts freelancers on payroll rather than having us invoice. I had mistakenly included it as part of my self-employed income. All of a sudden, I needed a letter of guarantee from the employer, stating who I am, my salary, etc, as if it were my main job.

Okay, I could do that. By when?

I knew I had to make *this* time work. We had paid out £3,000 for two visa applications already and I was worried I wouldn't have another £1,500 sitting around if this one got rejected.

We knew we couldn't appeal. Appeals are on hold until the MM human rights test case goes through, and the government are appealing the decision every step of the way. So, for the thousands on hold, it will take years, not months. We couldn't end up on that pile – not if we wanted to be together any time soon.

My heart sank as my husband read on: if we were to re-supply the information, it had to be at the Embassy by Monday at the latest. It was Wednesday. Could I get a package across Europe in time?

It turned out I could *if* I got the necessary information to the courier by Thursday. The woman on the other end of the phone was massively helpful once she understood the circumstances, and went far beyond the call of duty to help. I later found out that she'd had her own problems with UK visas and completely understood what was at stake.

It seems to me that every time we apply for a visa, we pack up all our hopes and dreams and wrap them up in the papers and the certificates. We send them off to the British Embassy and pray that this time our dreams will come true.

So I had 24 hours to assemble all the paperwork. I got the new letter and reassembled every single thing we had sent before. I figured it wouldn't to guarantee that the Officer had *everything* on the desk to look through while making a decision.

I don't remember much about those 24 hours. There was so much to do.

I ran about London, sometimes in tears, racing to get everything in time. I couldn't get hold of anyone in the Human Resources department at the organisation I had worked at, and I left message after message on the answerphones of pretty much everyone I knew who worked in that building, asking them to contact the specific person in HR. Every single one of those people got back to me and tried to help. It was successful. The next morning, the letter was waiting for me at Reception.

My accountant dropped everything to fit me in for a meeting on one of the busiest days of the tax year. His associate, who had helped us through the process of our second application, was there to support us. They both knew, from the previous application and subsequent rejection, how there seems to be a lack of training for the Officers who have to deal with a complex, self-employed application.

When I sent off the paperwork, I sent it with an eight-page letter, going through every single one of their list requirements, and explaining carefully, point by point, exactly which of the numbered documents fulfilled exactly what they were asking for.

And, at the end of the letter, I thanked the Officer for giving us the visa. I knew. I knew that this one would be successful and that my husband was finally coming home. I am a Buddhist, and I had been chanting for weeks for the Officer to lift their life state and to really have a heart connection with them.

I knew that my husband was coming home. He was coming home so that we could walk by the river, watch a movie, rub each other's feet. So that – finally – we could get our dog.

For me, that day, I knew that the Officer and I were finally able, in the face of this unjust law, to do some good. I knew that at least *one* family could finally be together.

I write this story with love for all those at the Home Office, and request that the Appeals stop and the law is changed. It is time for all the other families to finally be together, to come home each night to the people they love. To cook together, and eat together. To share birthdays and anniversaries around a table, not through a computer screen.

I request that we create the possibility of uniting families through a UK immigration system that has true integrity: an example for the whole world.

It is time.

**

**I arrived late. I hate being late; it's my Britishness.**

I'd been planning this trip to the airport for months, nearly a year, actually. It wasn't for lack of planning that I arrived late.

I could blame it on being a first-time mother. I still hadn't adjusted to how long it takes to do things, a common complaint from young women whose lives have changed. It's hard to transition from young professional with the world as one's oyster to simply trying to get out the door with clean clothes and the necessary items in relative harmony. Lip-gloss no longer makes the list.

I could also blame my tardiness on having to do it alone. There was no one to yell to:

"I'm just putting on a clean shirt. Can you please see that there is juice, nappies, and wipes in the bag?"

My husband would have swum the Atlantic to check on nappies, but that would've resulted in his deportation.

I could blame being late on the Monday Dublin rush-hour traffic. I had no idea that the thirty-minute commute would take an hour and a half. I had arrived in Dublin that morning on a rough ferry with toddler sick in my hair.

Olivia water-skied behind me on the smooth airport floor as

I considered possible reasons why my husband's flight could have been delayed, which would have made my lateness of no consequence. That list was discarded, incomplete and forgotten, the moment a shrill 'Papa' escaped my daughter's mouth. She'd seen him first. It was Papa, who she hadn't seen for the last five months – other than on Skype, when his on-call shifts allowed. He was more handsome than a 24-hour flight should've allowed. He smiled with relief and joy, no trace of 'Why are you late?'

The year's stress, anger, despair, and exhaustion vanished as I watched our little girl hurl herself at him, the man I worried she might not remember or be too nervous to let him hold her like the last time we had seen him. Five months previous, we had flown to Ecuador. An ear infection had taken hold on the 26-hour flight, and our little bubble of joy had faded, become thin, whiny, and scared.

But she was no longer the nervous, fragile infant I hid my tears from in the Ecuadorian airport, fixing my gaze on the departure sign, refusing to look back at my husband. I knew the pain I would find on his face would be too much for my stiff upper lip. In that dreadful departure, I chose not to turn and give my husband any signal of love his eyes were craving.

I regret that cold, stern walk away. In that one gesture of self-preservation, I thought only of myself. I thought about how I was going to get through the long flight home, alone, with a 17-month old. I thought about the jet-lag and sleepless nights that travelling and illness had made of our routine. The selfishness of those worries left no room to realise the far greater hurt and despair: I wasn't just leaving my husband – I was taking his daughter with me. Each minute of my daily struggle was a slap of stinging ingratitude in my husband's face because each time I had to get up to comfort our daughter was another moment he couldn't be there to father her.

But, in the Dublin airport, all of that seemed less unbearable. I walked over and put my arms around my little family and said:

"You've got the visa. I found out today. They've changed their minds and you've got the visa."

✽ ✽

On a cloudy day in April 2011, Tony Stephens, from Birmingham in the UK, was sent to me by E-Harmony as a match. When I first saw his picture, I told myself, 'No way, not a man with dreadlocks'. He sent me a message and mentioned that he used to work with BBC radio, which interested me. Soon, he started calling me in the Philippines.

A month later, I was on my way to the UK with my mother. I was excited to see my sister and her family, but I was also excited for myself: I was dreaming of finally meeting my match.

My first meeting with Tony was on a Saturday at a Starbucks in Nottingham city centre.

Tony arrived 15 minutes late and, for the second time, I was not impressed with his dreadlocks. He was over-confident and too easygoing. He smoked and swayed his dreadlocks, which he must have thought I would find attractive. When we later went to a bar, I immediately looked for the nearest exit just in case I needed to get out quickly.

On our way back to the city centre, I saw an open church and asked Tony if he would accompany me inside. He did and later told me he had prayed that we could be together some day. He left me by kissing me on my forehead, which I found unusual but sweet. Our first meeting had started with suspicion but ended with possibility.

My feelings for Tony kept getting stronger. He was funny, very natural, thoughtful, consistent, and caring. He became my constant companion in the UK.

There were lots of little things that made me fall in love with Tony:

When I was lost in London after taking the wrong train, I panicked. Tony called me every five minutes, guiding me all the way until I was safely home. He always made sure that I was safe when we were not together.

He had a natural ability to handle my childish tantrums; his patience was a calming presence that felt like a warm blanket.

His house was always clean and organised. Every room was spotless, which always impressed me.

He was a very good cook. 'Regular' food was improved by the Jamaican twists he would add to recipes. The first time he cooked for me, he made roasted lamb shoulder and black-eyed peas with rice.

Any lingering doubts I may have had disappeared when I met his family and friends. We had gathered for his cousin's birthday, and I was instantly made to feel welcome among his family. Tony's family was obviously important to him. He told me that most of the younger members of his family look after their parents and grandparents, and when a family member is in trouble, everyone rallies around to give support and help. I instantly felt at home amongst them.

The more time I spent with Tony, the more I fell in love with him. I enjoyed every minute with him. The way he showed his love was very natural. Sometimes we were like kids, holding hands while skipping on our way to the bus stop.

I eventually had to leave the UK to return home. He promised to meet me in Hong Kong a few months later on a business trip and to spend Christmas with me in my country. In October, we met in Hong Kong, where I introduced him to some of my friends. We spent our days eating, walking and laughing together.

December 25, 2011 was his first visit to my country. I was so happy when I met him at the airport. He spent two weeks' holiday in my country with my family. It was one of the happiest times of my life!

He came back to the Philippines for the second time and married me on July 18, 2012. It was a simple celebration at a Chinese restaurant attended by family members and close friends. One month after our wedding, he went back to the UK to continue working.

I applied for a settlement visa in September of 2012 to join my husband in the UK. We were refused because Tony did not meet the financial requirements. He had two jobs in the UK and I owned a small business in the Philippines. We planned to combine our joint income to support ourselves. It was never our intention to rely on the government for our upkeep. However, I was told that my business income from my country was not allowable.

For the third time, my husband came to the Philippines in December 2012 for a holiday. While he was here, his mother died, unexpectedly, on Christmas Day. He asked me to go with him to UK to bury his mother. I applied for a visitor's visa. Because of our pending settlement visa appeal, I was refused. He was devastated when he found out that I couldn't join him.

On 24 January 2013, Tony had a fatal heart attack while still in the Philippines. He had been due to return to the UK four days later to attend his mother's funeral. Again, I applied for a visitor's visa – this time to bury my husband. I was distraught when I was refused because the immigration officer thought I might overstay my visa.

Tony's two children from his previous relationship came to the Philippines for the funeral, and his ashes were brought back to the UK and buried with his mother on February 1, 2013.

When Tony was alive, I always wished, hoped that our goodbyes would end. We have said goodbye many times at train and bus stations in Nottingham, Euston, Birmingham, and London, and in the airports in Hong Kong and the Philippines.

Seeing his two children leaving me behind at the Philippine airport in order to bring his ashes back to the UK was the most painful feeling I ever felt in my life. That was my last goodbye to him – ashed Tony without reciprocal hugs and kisses.

After my settlement application was refused, I was made to feel like a criminal, penalized beyond my control. The refusal of a visa that would have allowed me to bury my husband felt inhumane and heartless. I thought consideration would be given to me for humanitarian reasons, but I was wrong. I am working on an appeal to see my late husband's grave. Over a year later, I am still grieving and left wondering if my late husband was a criminal for not being able to earn the money required by the Government.

Every day I pray that someone powerful in the UK will

understand what I am going through. I am hoping that person is compassionate – not only to me but also to many couples who are separated from their loved ones. And, hopefully, a miracle will happen.

\* \*

**After eighteen months of hell, I finally got the visa. I will never forget that moment. I have had many beautiful moments in my life, but none were better:**

It was Wednesday, a very sunny day in Podgorica, Montenegro. I was working with my friends when I got the message from the British Consulate. 'The decision about your visa is made. Please, can you come and collect your passport?'

My experiences of being turned down all the times before was that if they gave me a brown envelope I hadn't made it. It was the same situation this time, too. I was handed one big, brown envelope. As I collected it at the gate, before opening it, I told my best friend that I didn't have the visa. I signed a bunch of papers to confirm that I had collected my passport and then left.

We sat in the car for a few minutes. I was upset, angry – heartbroken. My best friend knew; he could see it on my face. He had been supporting my wife and I through the seemingly endless eighteen-month process. He said, 'Don't worry, together we are going to get through this – one day at a time.'

I opened the envelope. The first thing that came out was a CD of our wedding photos. It was strange that they sent this back to me because they had never returned it before. The next thing I saw was our marriage certificate. And then the certificate that I had passed the English exam in Belgrade. It was crazy to receive those documents, too, because they had never done that before either. And then I saw the certificate that I am a Citizen of Montenegro. That was when my heart came into my throat.

I opened my passport and saw the first visa, which was the Family Visitor holiday visa that we had managed to get eighteen months ago, just after we got married. On the next page was something yellow, brown, black, and blue.

Then I saw it. I saw the visa. In that moment, I shouted with joy. I called my wife. She cried with happiness.

At the end of all this is the message that together we can do anything. Beat every barrier. Beat every sadness. My wife and I could never have succeeded without the love and support of our families and friends. The message is that we didn't give up hope. The message is that we will never give up until everyone finds the thing that they are fighting for. And that is love.

# *Epilogue*

This book was created to document extraordinary moments in extraordinary relationships: the relationships of those who do not have the same human rights of the rest of the UK because of the 2012 Family Immigration Law.

Reading the book raises, for many, the question: *What can I do?*

The answer will change over time. UK laws evolve and change.

The most important thing that you can do is to talk about this. It is by talking and letting people know that we can create change. This situation has been under-reported and misreported in the mainstream press, but that is now changing. You can share about it on social media. You can blog about it. You can write articles about it. You can write letters. If you are in the position to do so, you can write policy and laws about it.

We support you in doing so.

We are committed to talking about this until every affected family is united.

Come join us, learn more at:

*www.loveletershome.org*

\*\*

*Love Letters to the Home Office was created by:*

# Letter Writers

| | |
|---|---|
| *Amanda* | *Jo* |
| *Anonymous* | *Joanne* |
| *Arlene* | *Jonathan* |
| *Carol* | *Katharine Rose* |
| *Chris* | *Kirsten* |
| *Daisy* | *Laura* |
| *David* | *Leslie-Jo* |
| *Dee* | *Lindsay* |
| *Fawzia* | *Lizzie Celi* |
| *Gillian* | *Lucy* |
| *Helen* | *Maddie* |
| *Iqqi* | *Nikkei* |
| *Jasmine* | *Oualid* |

## Ghost Writers

Paul

Raco

Rashila

Ren

Rohima

Rose Marie

Sam

Sandy

Sarah

Sion

Stella

Steph

Steven

Teresa

Toni

Alex

Julia

Katharine Rose

Kelli

Lily

Tonvanne

## Editor

David

## Creative Team

Abbi

David

Jason

Katharine Rose

Lightning Source UK Ltd.
Milton Keynes UK
UKOW05f0945190514

231911UK00017B/634/P